Note to Parents and Teachers

Once a reader can recognize and identify the 50 words used to tell this story, he or she will be able to successfully read the entire book. These 50 words are repeated throughout the story, so that young readers will be able to recognize the words easily and understand their meaning.

The 50 words used in this book are:

a	cake	jelly	sweet
about	cherries	know	the
all	chocolate	learned	things
always	cookies	like	to
and	day	lollipops	today
baking	doughnuts	made	too
be	eat	make	want
beans	favorite	Mother's	way
berries	have	my	what
big	hooray	neat	will
birthday	I	new	yummy
blue	is	not	
brownies	it	something	

Today is my birthday.

My Birthday Cake

Written by Olivia George

Illustrated by Martha Avilés

children's press ®

A Division of Scholastic Inc.

New York Toronto London Auckland Sydney
Mexico City New Delhi Hong Kong
Danbury, Connecticut

Library of Congress Cataloging-in-Publication Data

George, Olivia.
  My birthday cake / written by Olivia George ; illustrated by Martha Avilés.
     p. cm. — (My first reader)
  Summary: A little girl designs herself a birthday cake that has all her favorite ingredients, including jelly beans, cookies, muffins, lollipops, and more.
   ISBN 0-516-25178-3 (lib. bdg.)   0-516-25276-3 (pbk.)
   [1. Cake—Fiction. 2. Birthdays—Fiction. 3. Stories in rhyme. 4. Humorous stories.] I. Avilés Junco, Martha, ill. II. Title. III. Series.
   PZ8.3. G2945My 2005
   [E]—dc22
                                                                    2004010112

Published in 2005 by Children's Press, an imprint of Scholastic Library Publishing.
Published simultaneously in Canada.
Printed in the United States of America.

1 2 3 4 5 6 7 8 9 10 R 14 13 12 11 10 09 08 07 06 05

Hooray! Hooray!

My birthday is
always my favorite day.

I want something yummy.

I know what to make!

I want to make
a big birthday cake!

My cake will be yummy.

My cake will be sweet.

My cake will have
all the things I like to eat!

My cake will have cookies and
chocolate and berries.

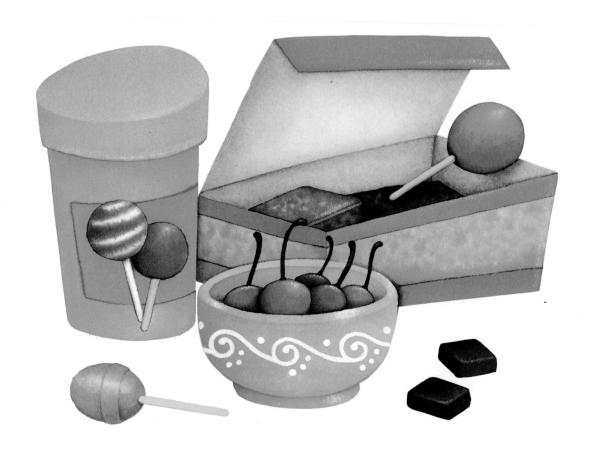

My cake will have lollipops,
brownies, and cherries.

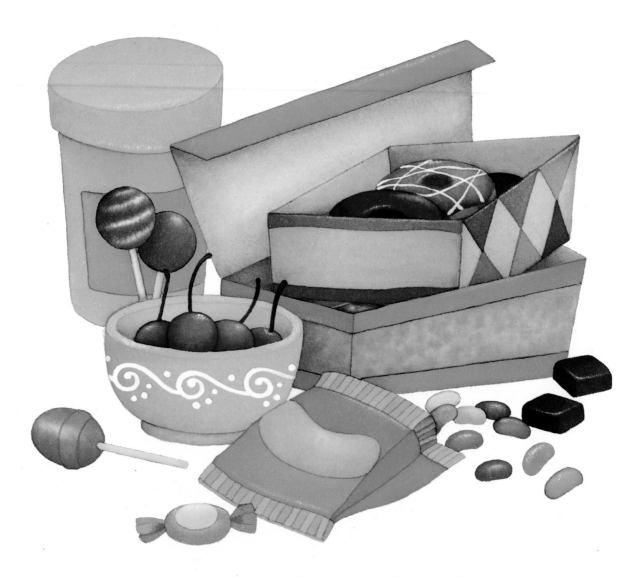

My cake will have doughnuts
and jelly beans, too.

My cake will be yummy.

My cake will be blue!

My cake is too blue!

My cake is not neat!

My cake is too big.

It is too sweet to eat!

I learned something new
about baking today.

The cake I want is
made Mother's way!

ABOUT THE AUTHOR

Olivia George was born and raised in a "children's book family" in Brooklyn, New York, and continues to carry on this tradition from her current home in Oakland, California. Olivia's love for cooking and baking was born around age eight, when she began making birthday cakes. *My Birthday Cake* is her second book with Children's Press.

ABOUT THE ILLUSTRATOR

Martha Avilés was born in Mexico City, where she now lives with her daughter. Avilés studied at the University of Mexico, and has been a full time illustrator since 1991, when her first book was published.